CW00516712

# Tiger Forest

## A Visual Study of Ranthambhore National Park

# Tiger Forest

## A Visual Study of Ranthambhore National Park

Chris Brunskill

Cheltenham Investments Ltd
Hong Kong
e-mail: chris@chrisbrunskill.co.uk

ISBN 1-920785-22-1



Typesetting and design: Troubador Publishing Ltd, Market Harborough, UK
Printed and bound by Everbest Printing Ltd, China

**For Kitty**

Chalo...

*When questing through the jungle the tiger glides silently along. He seems to flow past one like a phantom.*

**Dunbar Brander**

# Contents

*To hunt the tiger, you must first hunt the tiger in yourself, and to do that you first make certain that the tiger is not hunting you.*

**Mochtar Lubis**

# Foreword

As the head and founder of the Ranthambhore School of Art I have spent most of my life watching and painting the magnificent wild tigers for which Ranthambhore National Park is famous. My school promotes conservation through art, enhancing the appreciation and awareness of the area amongst both local people and foreign observers.

Working and training with local artists from the villages that surround the park, I, alongside my pupils, have developed a style of painting that reveals the true atmosphere of the forest. The great detail in which we paint is essential if we are to convey the distinctive beauty of Ranthambhore.

My goal as an artist is to take people into the forest through my work, experiencing the joy that I experience, hearing the sounds I hear. Art has the power to transport people, to evoke an echo inside of them, to speak to them. Chris Brunskill's photographs do this.

As an artist, I paint from the imagination, my dreams can become reality on canvas. A photographer has no such luxury, yet incredibly, this book contains images that I myself have dreamed of. A tiger on the edge of a cliff, an egret fishing from a sambar's nose, wild date palm trees at sunset and many more subtle interpretations of the jungle, all delicately infused with colour and contrast, light and shade, passion and drama.

As a photographer myself, I appreciate the immense patience and obsessive dedication that has been lavished on this portfolio. Tigers are elusive, wildlife is shy and landscapes often appear sullen. A photographer must work in these conditions and still capture rare seconds of drama, fleeting moments of wonder.

Many have come and gone from this remarkable place, however very few have illustrated in such detail, and with such skill, the beauty of this unique tiger forest like Chris Brunskill has in this stunning collection of images.

**MD Parashar**
**Ranthambhore School of Art**

*When you see a tiger, it is always like a dream.*

**Ullas Karanth**

# The Road to Ranthambhore

The single narrow track cuts through a gap in the mountain range that has towered above you since leaving the small town of Sawai Madhopur in the cover of darkness. During the journey, night quickly becomes day, and with the onset of another cold dawn comes an almost palpable air of expectancy. Sheer cliff faces loom over your passage through an ancient stone gate carved deep into the rocks. The road then rises sharply, you travel upwards for a time, before it eventually levels off. Emerging from the forest you are greeted with an expansive panorama.

Jungle stretches as far as the eye can see, mountains rise into the sky and the centrepiece of this spectacular landscape, a magnificent fortress, sits atop a huge rock. A stone sentinel overlooking the wilderness, as it has done at daybreak for a thousand years. Suddenly the road dips; with the wind rushing through your hair and the fresh forest air filling your lungs, you enter the National Park of Ranthambhore, the best place in the world to watch wild tigers.

I have had the good fortune of undertaking that same journey many times since glimpsing my first wild tiger here in December 1998. At the time I was a 21 year-old photography student seeking adventure and enlightenment; Ranthambhore was to exceed all of my expectations. Those early days were some of the most exciting of my life. Spellbound, I watched and photographed tigers stalking, walking in broad daylight along roads, killing prey and even turning up unannounced on the edge of cliffs. I was back just a couple of months later and over the years I've returned as often as possible, documenting the lives of several tigers and photographing the forest and all of its inhabitants.

This visual study is the result of those glorious times. In it I aim to celebrate the wonders of this tiger forest, in the process shedding some light on the lives of the animals that live in harmony with the tiger in this Indian wilderness.

Ranthambhore is one of the world's great National Parks. A veritable fantasy-forest where wild tigers roam around the remnants of a forgotten kingdom, amongst the souls of vanquished warriors. Its magic has seduced many over time and if you the viewer can feel just a little of that magic in my imagery then I will have accomplished my objectives with this book.

# Ranthambhore National Park

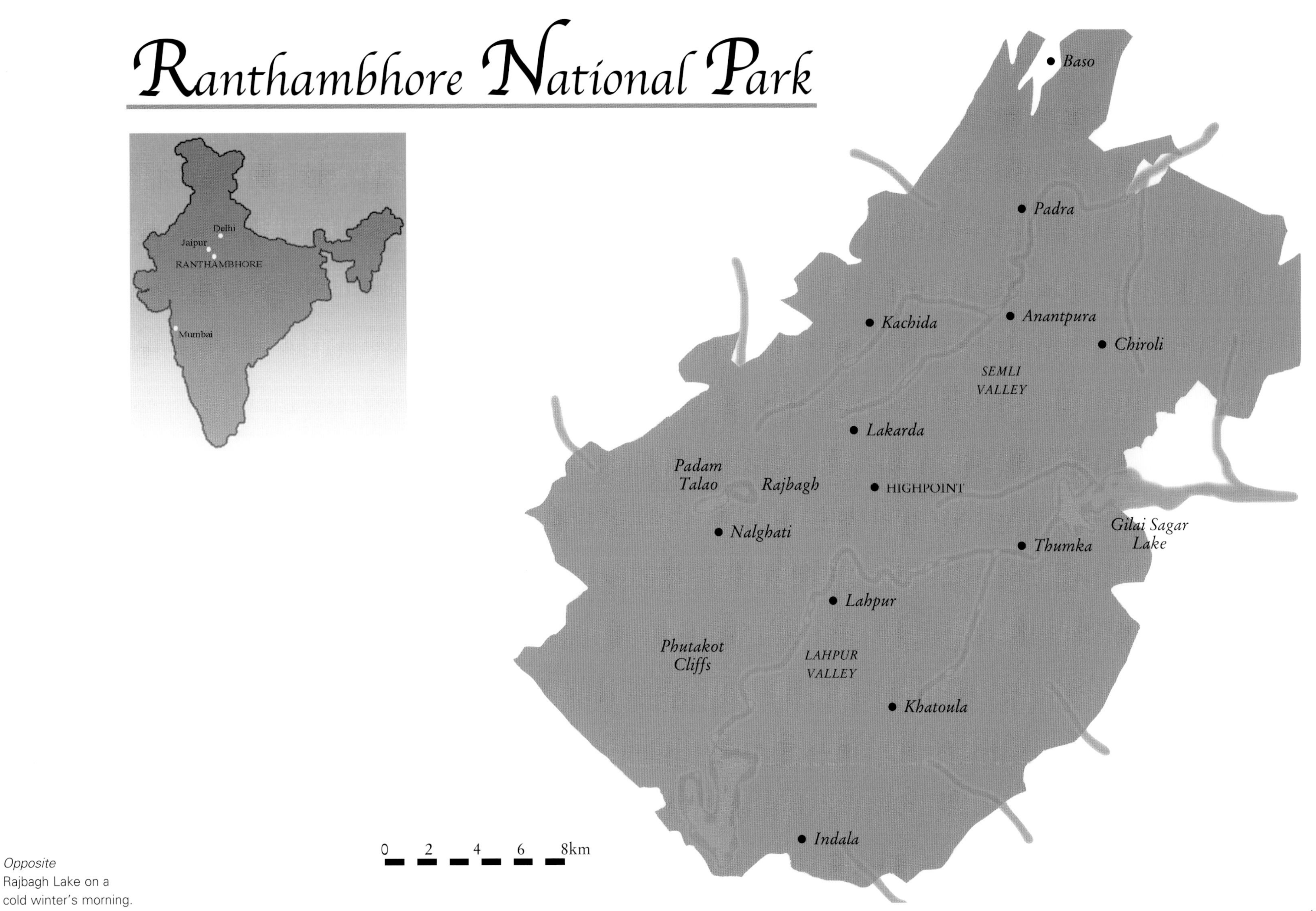


*Opposite*
Rajbagh Lake on a cold winter's morning.

# Tigers

Ranthambhore National Park is renowned as the best place in the world to watch wild tigers. Naturally fearful of man, tigers are so elusive in most parts of their range that many forest guards, people who live and work in tiger reserves, have had only a few fleeting encounters with these majestic cats during a lifetime's service.

Ranthambhore is different. Relatively open in nature, its forests offer a greater degree of visibility than that found anywhere else. Due in the most part to the strict protection offered them, certain tigers have gradually become accustomed to being observed by people in open jeeps.

This tolerance of people has, in the last twenty years, made Ranthambhore a paradise for naturalists, photographers and film-makers. In fact, much of what human beings have learned about wild tigers has been recorded here for the first time.

Despite all of these advantages, finding tigers is still far from easy. Days, even weeks, can pass without so much as a glimpse of a cat. Patience is a pre-requisite when searching for predators, and the waiting – while agonising at times – is an essential part of the process. For when it eventually comes, an encounter with a wild tiger – on its own terms, in its own landscape – is one of the most exhilarating experiences on earth.

*Bumbu Ram*
This large male tiger patrolled the forest for years, fathering several litters of cubs, before mysteriously disappearing. It is the males like Bumbu Ram who provide some of the most exciting moments in the forest. Wide-ranging and generally intolerant of human observers, male tigers often retreat into dense cover when sighted. They have a totally different demeanour to the females, and their baleful stare can be quite unnerving, especially when received at close quarters. Here Bumbu Ram lounges regally on a rock after missing a sambar deer by inches.

*Opposite*
Nick, a young male, stands majestically in the golden grass just before sunset. Male tigers are easily distinguishable from the females, being stockier and generally heavier set.

*Tiger on the road, Tambakhan*
Tigers frequently use the roads in Ranthambhore to patrol their well-defined territories. Possessing scent glands in their feet, walking along the tracks helps demarcate a tiger's home range as they wander through the forest.

*Opposite*
The tiger lives in a world of sunlight and shadow. Resting in the dappled forest light, the tiger's camouflage renders it almost invisible. There have been countless times when, from a distance, I have been looking right at a tiger but have been unable to see it. For me this picture evokes visions of the tiger as a ghost-like presence. A mysterious, cryptic hunter roaming the deep valleys of the forest in search of prey.

*Tiger listening*
Tigers have excellent hearing and can pick up sounds that human beings cannot detect. This enhanced hearing is one of the reasons why tigers are so elusive in most forests. Those not habituated to human beings can hear intruders well before they can be seen, and they then simply get up and walk away. This young tigress seemed to be trying to locate something in the nala 300–400ft below.

*Opposite*
Machali, the resident tigress of the lakes, rests at dusk on a dried up Malik Talao, the smallest of Ranthambhore's three lakes. Malik Talao is usually completely dry by April or May, when this picture was taken. With no-one else around we stayed with Machali in the fading light as she lay, in typical tiger fashion, with the head over the front paws, on the green lake bed.

# The Hunt

*The tigress lies flat across the track in front of us. Her concentration is locked onto the herd of chital that graze, unaware of her presence, just 40ft away. Ears turned forward, eyes focused, every muscle in her sleek body is taught, tense; ready for the final, explosive charge she has been inching closer to for almost twenty minutes.*

*Heart in my mouth, I see her expression change a millisecond before the charge. She races across the road with murderous intent, bursting into the herd. Closing in, she makes a final lunge and her paw grazes the rear leg of a young fawn, sending it spinning. Ruthlessly clamping her jaws on the back of its neck, the deer's life ends swiftly as the tigress' dagger-like canines severe its spinal cord.*

Watching a tiger hunting is to witness the pinnacle of predatory evolution, an innate instinct that has been developed, honed and perfected over the course of its life. The concentration is total, the focus unwavering. You can see them thinking, calculating, contemplating – deciphering signals and stimuli, using years of experience to time their strikes successfully.

Formidable predators, tigers are capable of bringing down prey two or three times their own size. No other land animal attacks and kills larger prey, on a one-on-one basis, than the tiger. Equipped with powerful forelimbs, razor sharp claws and dagger-like canine teeth, the tiger is heavily armed and fears nothing in the natural world except other tigers and, with good reason – man.

*Tiger stalking*
Crouching low to the ground, the shoulder blades become the highest point of a tiger's body when it's stalking prey. This tigress froze when the antelope she was approaching stopped grazing and lifted its head from the ground

A chital flees as Machali strolls across the shore of Padam Talao. Chital are the most numerous of the tiger's prey species in Ranthambhore. There is a "safe zone" around a herd of deer that are watching a tiger. While the tiger is outside of this zone they will call in alarm and stamp their feet, alerting their fellow creatures to the danger. As soon as the tiger gets too close and enters the zone, as in this picture, they will flee. It is wonderful to observe at first hand the effect the tiger has on the forest as it, in famous words, "spreads its dread".

Two tigers stalk a group of sambar drinking from a waterhole at dusk. Co-operative hunting like this has been observed before, but in most cases it has been a mother and her adolescent cubs. Here an unrelated male and female are in the initial stages of a stalk that saw both of them approach from opposite sides of the deer, reminiscent of a lion's "pincer" attack. Like many hunts, it was ultimately unsuccessful.

Tigers often hide kills and return to feed over several days. This large sambar stag could provide a single tiger with food for 3–5 days. The tiger has taken a few bites out of the left foreleg and then probably went to rest up in the vicinity of the carcass, although we never saw it.

Tigers take infinite care when stalking prey. They flatten their bodies low to the ground to minimise their profile in an approach that can take upwards of an hour. Here we see Machali within range of a group of wild boar and ready to charge.

She bursts forward, the colour of her coat changing as she moves from the shadows into the morning light.

Although frozen in the pictures she is moving at great speed, covering the distance between herself and the boar in about 4 seconds. Unfortunately she just missed, possibly due to inexperience. Tigers are only occasionally successful, failing many more times than they succeed.

*Opposite*
Machali drags the wild boar into long grass. After killing, tigers move their victims to a secluded spot, away from the attention of scavengers, which can include vultures, smaller birds, jackals, hyenas and other tigers.

Machali choking a small wild boar piglet. Tigers strangle their prey with a vice-like throat hold, their powerful jaw muscles ensuring that the canine teeth are held firmly in place as they deliver the lethal bite. While strangulation is the most common killing technique, tigers also bite the nape of their prey, breaking the neck.

*Tigress with freshly killed sambar, Bakola*
This tigress has brought down a fairly large sambar. We first noticed the carcass early one morning and, like hunters in bygone years, returned later in the day, anticipating the tiger's return. After several hours the forest erupted in a cacophony of alarm calls, and the tigress made a grand entrance, perfectly befitting the lord of the forest. It has been repeatedly observed in Ranthambhore that tigers don't like to be watched while feeding. As you can see from her stare, she is uncomfortable with our presence.

*Opposite*
Sambar skeleton, Kachida. Sambar are the tiger's favourite prey in Ranthambhore. Here a large stag has been killed and eaten by a tiger; the skeleton was then stripped bare by scavengers, leaving only the skull and spine behind. This will eventually be broken down and return peacefully to the forest from where it came, in the endless cycle of life and death that regulates all tiger forests.

# Ranthambhore

The area we now call Ranthambhore National Park has a fascinating past that can be traced back a thousand years to when the fortress of Ranthambhore, from which the area takes its name, was constructed. For centuries Ranthambhore Fort was claimed, conquered and fought over by armies of men under the control of an impressive array of emperors and kings, including, in a celebrated assault, Akbar the Great.

In more recent times, the Ranthambhore forests came under the jurisdiction of the Maharajahs of Jaipur, who indulged in their love of hunting in the area. Their passion for shooting tigers aside, the Maharajahs respected nature and generally protected the forests. Hunting was only permitted during a specific period, which allowed new tigers to take the place of those that were killed during the short shooting season.

Today, echoes of these times past have merged with the reserve's sublime beauty to create an area of splendid wilderness, uniquely embellished by both nature and man. The forest around the three lakes in the centre of the park contains spectacular landscapes; dotted here and there with crumbling ruins, summer palaces, guard posts and temples. It is these remnants of conflict and royalty, surrounded by wild date palms and banyan trees, that create the area's exotic charm and lie, alongside the tiger, at the heart of Ranthambhore's mystique.

*Wild date palm tree at sunset.*

*Opposite*
Sunset over Ranthambhore. This is the stunning view from the top of the nearby Khandar Fort that lies on the eastern edge of the forest.

Rajbagh Lake with the summer palace, a legacy of a royal history, nestled on the far side.
Machali, the resident tigress of the lakes, often used this crumbling palace to hide her young cubs during their first few months of life.

A peacock displays in front of a chatri. These ruins are spread throughout the forest, giving Ranthambhore a mystique that few places possess.

From a rise, Ranthambhore Fort can be seen spectacularly jutting out from the forest canopy. It must have been an imposing sight for the armies of men who have laid siege to it down the centuries.

*Opposite*
Padam Talao. This lake lies directly beneath the fort. The small island you see is the permanent perch of scores of cormorants in winter.

Rajbagh Lake.

A sambar stag feeds in the rich waters of Rajbagh Lake.

Considered sacred by Hindus, banyan trees can live for hundreds of years. This is reportedly one of the biggest in India.

Banyan Tree, Jalhra.

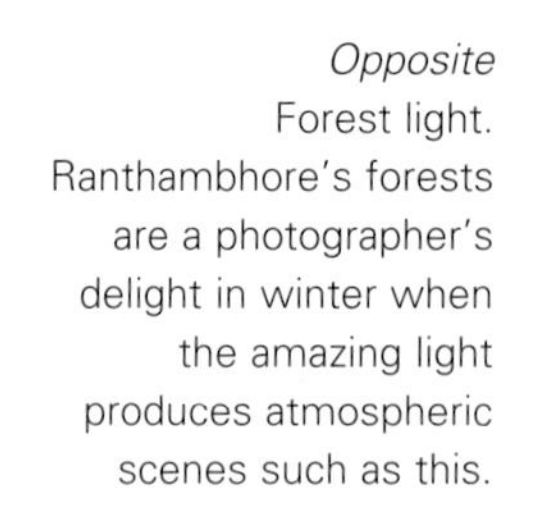

*Opposite*
Forest light. Ranthambhore's forests are a photographer's delight in winter when the amazing light produces atmospheric scenes such as this.

# Tiger Territory

In February 2001 I was witness to an extraordinary sequence of events involving the tigress Machali and a young male tiger called Nick.

At the time Machali was successfully raising her cubs around the lakes. The father of her cubs, Bumbu Ram, had mysteriously disappeared soon after mating, leaving Machali and her offspring alone and unprotected.

This was potentially a very dangerous situation, as a new male that comes into the area will often kill a mother's cubs to bring the tigress into oestrus. This enables him to sire his own progeny and extend his bloodline. Without Bumbu Ram to protect them, Machali's family was highly vulnerable, and Nick, a young male from Kachida, offered the greatest threat.

We constantly found him patrolling the lakes, following the same routes day after day, leaving his scent in the same areas. Machali, clearly agitated and recognising the threat, was doing the same, and continuously roaring as she travelled through her territory. Her cubs then became very elusive as she wisely hid them in the most inaccessible of areas, away from our eyes and, more importantly, away from Nick's.

Eventually the two would meet, but would it be too late for Machali and her cubs?

Nick, the resident male tiger of the lakes area, defecates on the road. This scat, alongside the scent that is left with it, will confirm to any passing tigers that this territory is occupied. After depositing the scat Nick scraped dirt off the road onto it with his hind legs. This is thought to preserve its pungent odour for longer.

Machali, the resident tigress of the lakes, patrolling her territory. I was witness to her initial confrontation with a young Nick in Febuary 2001. Here she is returning at dusk from a long journey through her home range.

Machali would constantly roar and scent mark every hundred yards, appearing clearly agitated. It was a great thrill to hear a tiger's roar so frequently. Unlike lions, who communicate with their pride members by roaring at night, tigers are far less vocal due to their solitary nature.

*Nick Scent Marking*
Tigers raise their tail and squirt the base of trees, rocks or any other prominent landmarks with a stream of fluid. This fluid is a mixture of urine and scent secretion from the anal glands, and its strong pungent odour will linger for weeks. It is this behaviour that allows tigers to lead a largely solitary existence yet still communicate effectively, avoiding potentially dangerous face to face confrontations with their neighbours.

Here he rubs the scent glands in his cheek high on a branch. Any passing tiger smelling this odour will be able to tell how long ago it was left, the sex of the tiger, and they may even be able to identify individuals by their distinctive scent.

Machali smells the tree and then applies a stream of her own scent. She has rightly recognised Nick's presence in the area as a threat and by patrolling, roaring and scent marking she is asserting her territorial rights. A confrontation seems inevitable...

Eventually, through smell and sound, the two tigers locate each other. Machali at the rear, the older of the two, more than held her own in the face of the threat posed by this young, inexperienced male. On this day she stayed with Nick at all times, moving where he moved, resting where he rested. If he appeared to be heading back towards the lakes where her cubs were hidden, she would growl at him, warning him away.

Amazingly the day ended with both of them simultaneously stalking a group of sambar. Remarkable behaviour, and a clear sign that there is so much that we don't yet know about the mysterious lives of wild tigers. It was a very interesting episode and a wonderful time to be in the reserve observing true, natural behaviour.

*Epilogue*

Machali eventually repelled Nick's advances long enough for her cubs to gain their independence. After they had left her she immediately mated with Nick, and her second litter of cubs were born several months later.

# Denizens

Around 30 species of mammals find sanctuary within Ranthambhore National Park. From the squirrel to the sambar deer, each and every one occupies a vital niche in the reserve's complex ecological system and contributes to the forest's health and vitality.

## Herbivores

Of the herbivores, spotted deer (or chital) and sambar are the most abundant, and form a large part of the tiger's diet. Chital gather in fairly large herds to feed, while the larger sambar tend to be less gregarious, and are mainly found in small groups or alone.

Wild boar are a common sight around the lakes and in the more open areas, where they gather to feed in large groups called sounders. A large male boar is a fearsome sight, and they have been known to aggressively chase away inexperienced tigers

## Primates

Common or Hanuman langurs are seen all over the forest. Frequently found close to human settlements, langurs are adept at snatching food from the people who come to worship inside the fort in the centre of the reserve. Like all monkeys they are social creatures, and travel in large troops that can be amusing to watch. Justifiably afraid of the tiger, they bark in alarm whenever they catch a glimpse of one, often helping to locate the big cats.

## Co-Predators

The tiger's co-predators include leopards, hyenas, crocodiles and jackals. Leopards are rarely encountered, and mainly stick to the outskirts of the forest where they prey on all manner of creatures, including the occasional stray dog. Mugger crocodiles are a menacing sight in the lakes and rivers – large adults can grow up to four metres long, and are more than capable of killing large animals such as sambar.

Hyenas, like leopards, are elusive, due in the most part to their solitary, nocturnal habits. Jackals are also creatures of the night, retiring to their dens before dawn. Their long mournful calls are occasionally heard piercing the early morning air.

Another fascinating creature native to Ranthambhore is the sloth bear. Covering tremendous distances at night, they forage for food between dusk and dawn, feeding mainly on fruit and insects.

## Avian Fauna

Almost 300 species of birds have been recorded in the reserve, nearly a quarter of those found in the whole of the Indian Sub-Continent.

Birds of prey patrol the skies, feeding upon small mammals, birds and, in the case of one specialist, snakes. Vultures soar high on the thermals, their keen eyes scanning the jungle for their next feast. Five species of owl thrive here, shadow-like presences in the night air.

Cattle egrets and pond herons, chauffeured by sambar deer, fish from their welcoming hosts in the rich waters of the lakes, and painted storks, with their dazzling plumage, add to the beauty of the surroundings.

Smaller birds of bewildering hues and colours flit through the trees. Exotic parakeets are a common sight, phenomenal aerialists; they hurtle through the forest canopy, dodging twigs and branches as if guided by radar. Rufous treepies, small scavenging birds, are attracted to carcasses, frequently provoking enraged tigers as they peck at their kills.

Peacocks, the national bird of India, add more splendour, regally displaying during a majestic courtship unmatched in the natural world. Often the first indication of a tiger, their calls are one of the truly evocative sounds of the Indian jungle.

*Opposite*
Langurs live throughout India, and after human beings have the largest distribution of all primates.

*Spotted Deer*
These abundant deer are also known as chital.

The fleet footed chinkara or Indian gazelle is a small antelope occasionally seen in the more open areas of the forest.

*Nilgai*
Considered sacred, their name translates as 'blue cow', nilgai are often found outside of protected areas. Ranthambhore is a particularly good place to see them.

Wild boars are omnivorous and will occasionally feed on carrion. Here this boar is feeding on a chital, aided by a crow. Crows are just one of a number of scavenging birds that feed from kills, although a tiger, unlike the boar in this picture, would not accept their presence at a feast.

Sambar

Sambar drinking.

Sambar wallowing in the muddy shoreline of Rajbagh Lake.
I watched this stag for nearly an hour as he caked himself in mud in the heat of the afternoon.

*Opposite*
Sambar and cattle egret.
The egrets use the sambar as mobile platforms and regularly fly between individuals in a herd, depending on their position in the lake.

*Egret fishing off sambar stag's nose*
The sambar are incredibly tolerant of the cattle egrets that use them as perches. This stag even allowed the egret to walk down its head and fish from the end of its nose.

*Two young sambar stags spar*
Essentially play, this instinct amongst these young deer will develop as they get older. In later life stags engage in powerful battles with rival males in disputes over mating rights.

# Chital

A herd of chital graze on the edge of Rajbagh Lake. Congregating in large herds provides greater protection from predators as more pairs of eyes and ears can pinpoint danger.

*Chital and fawn*
Young chital stay very close to their mothers in the early stages of life.

*Chital in velvet*
Velvet is a furry, external skin that covers and nourishes a deer's antlers as they grow. It eventually falls or is rubbed off by the deer when they have fully grown.

*Spotted deer fleeing from a tiger*
After calling in alarm several times this spotted deer fled when a tiger approached to within 30–40ft.

Chital and langurs are often found together. Here the deer pays particular attention to the langur's long tail.

Chital fawns.

# Hanuman Langurs

Worshipped across India, langurs are considered sacred by Hindus, who view them as living incarnations of the monkey god Hanuman.

*Langur and Wild Boars*
The langur and wild boar, like the chital, are often found together. Langurs are messy feeders and drop fruits to the ground, where large groups of wild boar gather to feed on them. The langurs also serve as a lookout, and they will bark in alarm if they catch sight of an approaching predator.

*Langur running*
Langurs can run at quite a speed, and appear to take great delight in crashing around on the ground with fellow members of the troop.

*Langur and baby drinking*
Within minutes of being born, young langurs are passed among the troop.

Mother and young stare quizzically at the camera as the juvenile suckles.

*Opposite*
This baby grabs the nipple, indicating he wants to be fed. Baby langurs will occasionally suckle from other females in the troop as well as their mothers.

A langur keeps a watchful eye out from the treetops. In the branches they move with great speed and agility, and are capable of making massive jumps between trees.

Langurs spend a lot of their time on the ground, although they retreat to the treetops at the first hint of danger.

They consider themselves safe in the trees, although on the fringes of the forest leopards will venture into the treetops to take them. Young langurs are also, on rare occasions, preyed upon by the larger birds of prey.

# Co-Predators

## Leopard

Ranthambhore's leopards are rarely seen. I have only encountered these beautiful cats on two occasions during my study. Nocturnal by nature, their elusive ways can in part be attributed to their well-founded fear of the tiger.

Tigers will attack, kill and eat leopards if given the opportunity, viewing them as a danger to their cubs and competitors for food. Because of this they tend to stick to the outskirts of the park, and are highly opportunistic, preying on a variety of natural prey and, at times, livestock and stray dogs.

I had one fortunate extended observation of a leopard on a scorching summer's afternoon in the Nalghati Valley:

> *Rounding a bend in the forest a leopard sprints across the track in front of my jeep. Climbing up a rocky hill adjacent to the road, it turns to face me from a distance of 20 metres. The leopard rests, panting heavily and staring right into my camera lens. It continues to stare, and I am bemused as to why it is hanging around for so long.*
>
> *Turning around for the first time I see the reason. A half-dead spotted deer is lying fatally injured in a clearing 10 metres off the road on the other side, forlornly kicking its legs as two small scavenging birds begin pecking at its eyes. I must have surprised the leopard as it had caught the deer, and it had nervously taken flight as I approached.*

Truly fascinating behaviour that shows leopards are extremely cautious when hunting in prime tiger territory. Even though it had caught and killed a spotted deer, it was prepared to run away and give up its hard-earned meal just because my jeep had appeared on the scene.

> *Quickly deciding that I should move on and allow the leopard to claim its prize, I tell my driver to reverse back around the bend. In an instant the forest echoes with alarm calls – quickly accelerating forward, I return to the kill-site to find both the leopard and the carcass gone! In less than 20 seconds the leopard had sprinted down the hill, grabbed the carcass and concealed itself in the time it took to reverse back and then accelerate forward around the bend.*

It was an amazing sequence of events, one that offered a tantalising window into the world of Ranthambhore's secretive leopards.

*Opposite*
Leopard, Nalghati.

*Sloth Bear, Kachida*
Sloth bears were erroneously given their name by early explorers who believed them to be true sloths. They were initially called bear sloths – only when the truth was discovered did they become known as the sloth bear.

*Opposite*
Sloth Bear, Lakarda
Omnivorous, sloth bears feed mainly on termites, fruits and honeycomb, although they will eat carrion. They have several interesting adaptations that allow them to eat termites, including nostrils that they can seal up ensuring nothing crawls inside their nose. Their long hairless muzzle is poked deep into termite mounds, sucking out large numbers of insects in a similar fashion to anteaters.

They have a fearsome reputation, and are considered extremely bad tempered. Many humans have been savagely injured or maimed by them on the fringes of the park, including several forest guards.

*Mugger's crocodiles are found in Ranthambhore's lakes and rivers*
Artificially introduced in the late 1970s, adults can grow up to four metres long.
A fearsome sight lounging on the lake shore, they prey on a variety of creatures, including the occasional sambar deer.

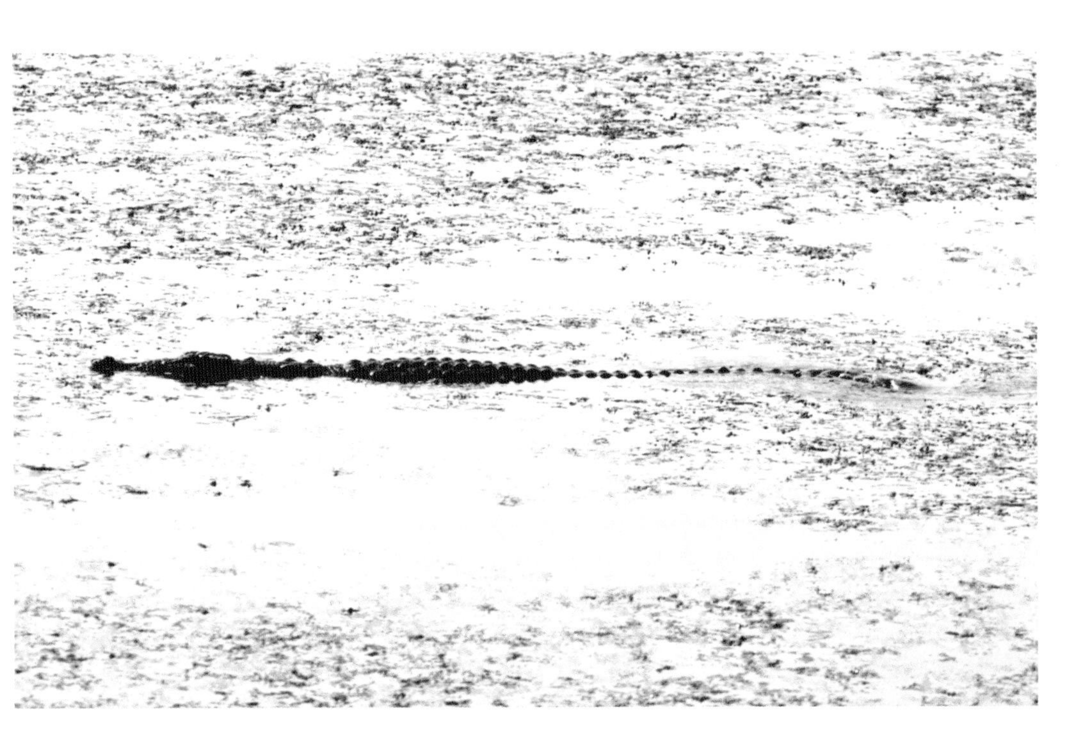

*Mugger in Padam Talao*
Superbly designed, crocodiles can hide below the surface of the water with only their eyes and nostrils visible. This adaptation allows them to approach unwary prey without being detected.

*Crocodile Sunbathes*
Being cold-blooded, crocodiles need the sun's rays to raise their body temperature. They are often seen basking on the lakeshore in the early afternoon when the sun is at its hottest.

*Jackal feeding on a chital carcass*
On the whole scavengers, jackals will occasionally hunt chital fawns.

*Opposite*
Desert Monitor Lizard.

*Peacock displaying*
Peacocks are the national birds of India and, like many creatures, are revered in Hindu myth and legend. They display their spectacular tail feathers to attract the attention of peahens.

*Opposite*
This shikra has just killed a crow pheasant.

*Crested Serpent Eagle*
As their name suggests, these birds prey heavily on snakes. They are often found around the lakes, watching for any sign of disturbance in the water with their keen eyes.

*Opposite*
Oriental Honey Buzzard, Bakola. Honey buzzards are found mainly in heavily wooded forest.

*Opposite*
A painted stork flies over Padam Talao at dusk.

*Woolly-Necked Stork*
Woolly or white-necked storks are often seen in the lakes.

*Painted Stork*
Painted storks are another common sight. Widely distributed over the whole of India, a large population of these birds nest in the nearby Keoladeo National Park at Bharatpur.

*Little Cormorants, Padam Talao*
Groups containing 20–30 little cormorants fly around the edge of Padam Talao in winter, occasionally with a bird of prey in hot pursuit.

*Black Drongo*
Sleek black birds with a distinctive forked tail, black drongos are found both alone and in groups.

Common myna hitching a ride on a sambar stag.

*Stork-Billed Kingfisher*
Ranthambhore is home to several species of kingfishers. Beside fish, kingfishers eat insects, frogs, lizards and small rodents. After seizing large prey they then take it back to their perch, where it is often whacked to death.

*Eurasian Thick-knee*
Thick-knees derive their name from their thickened tarsal joints. Shy and solitary, with their dull colours they blend well into dry landscapes.

*Opposite*
Indian Night-Jar. Heavily camouflaged, this Indian night-jar let me approach very close, believing itself to be invisible.

*Rufous Treepie*
Treepies are beautiful birds that are often found in the vicinity of tiger kills. Not fond of sharing, tigers will charge at them if they land anywhere near their kill.

*Red-Wattled Lapwing*
A variety of wading birds frequent the lakes.

# Machali - Life by the Lakes

Machali was the first wild tiger I ever saw. I remember it so vividly, so clearly, it might have happened yesterday. She was lying imperiously across the track that bisects Malik Talao late one winter's afternoon, blocking the traffic and totally at ease in our presence.

At the time she was an adolescent approaching independence, and just a few months after my first memorable encounter she challenged her mother for possession of the lakes. A fierce fighter, Machali suprisingly took control of the area after several aggressive confrontations, becoming the undisputed ruler of this prime tiger territory.

The lakes area in Ranthambhore is one of the most unique habitats in the world. It would be fair to say that no other tiger on earth lives in a place of such charm or splendour. Breathtakingly beautiful, these lakeside forests are also relatively open, making Machali more visible than other tigers. This exposure to people has resulted in her being completely relaxed in the presence of people observing her from vehicles.

Machali is a very pretty tigress, with exquisite facial markings. Easily recognisable, she has featured in 80% of my observations of Ranthambhore's tigers. Her beauty aside, Machali is a competent huntress who, like all tigers, must subdue and kill large, dangerous prey every few days to survive. Besides the deer that make up the vast majority of her diet, she has also been observed attacking crocodiles on dry land.

Her skills as a mother were tested early on in her life as she was forced to confront an aggressive male tiger that sought to mate with her after the disappearance of the father of her first litter, Bumbu Ram. Showing experience that belied her tender age, she managed to keep him at a safe distance from her offspring until they had matured and moved on to forge new lives for themselves in a different part of the forest.

*Opposite*
Machali, for once, gazes at the camera.

Machali was born in March/April 1997 in a litter of three female cubs. Like all tigers, she spent around two years in her mother's care, before eventually driving her from the lakes territory and claiming it for herself. After mating with the tiger Bumbu Ram in May 2000, she gave birth to her first litter of cubs in August of that year.

An all male duo – one had a distinctive kink in its tail and was aptly named Broken Tail – they were to be raised without the protection of their father, who mysteriously disappeared before they were born. Machali was then involved in constant conflict with Nick, a male tiger that sought to mate with her, putting the cubs in great danger.

Her two sons eventually left their mother in the spring of 2002, forging new territories on the fringes of the forest. Immediately after their departure, Machali mated with Nick, and gave birth to a litter of three cubs in May 2002. One sadly died early, leaving behind a male and female pair.

After this tragedy her second experience of motherhood proved to be a lot smoother. With Nick in his rightful role as father and protector, the two cubs had a secure family structure in place, and subsequently prospered.

# Family Tree

Machali, born March/April 1997

Bumbu Ram

Nick

Two cubs, born August 2000

Three cubs born May 2002, one died early

Broken Tail

Slant Ear

Male Cub

Female Cub

Macahli's second litter of cubs have not been named and will be called simply male and female cub in subsequent pages

Slant Ear at approximately six months old.

*Opposite*
Machali and Broken Tail walk along the shore of Rajbagh Lake at dawn. On this morning Slant Ear, her second cub, was missing and Machali was roaring to help the young tiger locate his family. The roars echoed off the Rajbagh Palace and could be genuinely mistaken for those of another tiger roaring back.

*Opposite*
Machali's family cross from Mandook into Jalhra, a small patch of thick forest which lies below the fort.

*Broken Tail*
As his name suggests, Broken Tail has a strange kink in his tail.

*Opposite*
Walking to Nalghati. In the heat of April we found Machali and her second litter every day heading down into the Nalghati Valley to rest in a series of caves that provide a cool shelter away from the oppressive heat of summer.

Machali drinking.

*Male cub, Jalhra*
At sunset the male cub lies beneath Ranthambhore Fort.

As Machali's male cub yawns a swarm of flies leaves their resting place on the end of his nose.

*Opposite*
Machali's 11 month-old female cub. Female cubs tend to be a lot shyer than their brothers. Interestingly, this changes as they grow older, when it is the mature male tigers that don't appear to appreciate their human observers.

Machali and her male cub rest at the bottom of a valley, directly below the Ranthambhore Fort.

*Machali's family lie across the track*
Machali and her cubs came up onto the vehicle track as the sun was rising over the steep cliffs of the Nalghati Valley, presenting me with a rare opportunity to fit the whole family into the frame.

One cub dominates his siblings in a litter, usually a male. Machali's second litter was no different, and her male cub dominated his smaller, shyer sister. This domination is apparent from an early age, and will continue until the cubs gain independence. The dominant cub has many advantages in the early years of its life, including getting first right to feed from kills and prime access to their mother's milk. The dominant cub is also considerably bolder, and while Machali's son would lie out in the open with her, her daughter often stayed hidden in thick cover.

In this sequence we see how intolerant tigress' can be of their cubs. As they grow older they increasingly leave them alone, rest up away from them and snarl, seemingly to discourage close contact. This is thought to be the beginning of the process that will see them reach independence, and is the tigress' way of getting them accustomed to a solitary life.

Machali playfully bites the nape, then snarls as the cub scampers off. He seemed to have heeded the warning and stayed away from his mother as they rested in the caves located in the Nalghati Valley.

This sequence shows a more frightening level of intolerance, and it shocked me to see Machali direct such fury at her own cubs.

After the female cub sits down next to her, Machali snarls in annoyance.

She jumps up, growls fiercely and then strikes the 11 month-old cub with her powerful forepaw.

Continuing to snarl, she walks off, leaving her cubs alone on the track. It remains a mystery to me why Machali behaved in this way. Maybe her offspring had irritated her before she came back onto the track seeking to be left alone. When they followed she was possibly annoyed that the female cub lay almost on top of her. This is a natural reaction amongst young cubs, who constantly seek reassurance from their mother while being observed.

Machali snarls at her male cub.

When the cubs are a respectful distance from her, Machali appears quite content, protectively watching over her offspring like every good mother should.

# Tigers: A Wild Future?

### Dominance

At the start of the 20th century 100,000 tigers roamed the planet. Their territory extended from the Russian Far East to the Caspian Sea, from the foothills of the Himalayas to the western isles of the Indonesian Archipelago.

The tiger was abundant, and existed in a bewildering array of habitats covering a great swath of Asia. Its influence on the people who shared its forests was profound. Tigers were worshipped as lord, protector and spirit of the forests, and anyone caught harming one was punished. Man lived in peaceful harmony with the great cats, and this respect for life ensured the tiger was the dominant creature of South Asia, the unchallenged ruler of all it surveyed.

### A Bloody Century

Sadly, a harmony that had evolved over thousands of years was shattered in the century that followed. The advent and proliferation of firearms after two bloody world wars found tigers in the sights of an ever-increasing number of hunter's guns. India's tigers in particular were hunted to such an extent that as early as 1944 Jim Corbett, famed killer of man-eating tigers and leopards, was warning of their rapidly reducing numbers.

His warning was not heeded. Tigers continued to vanish from large parts of their range, and the species, faced with a technologically superior opponent in man, was in grave danger of extinction. By the 1970s it was clear that drastic action was required, as there were thought to be less than 2000 tigers in the whole of India. Conservationists lobbied the government to do something about this looming catastrophe, and in 1973 Project Tiger was launched.

### Project Tiger

Project Tiger focused on strict protection of the tiger's habitat. Hunting was banned, interference was prohibited, and local villagers were ordered to re-settle outside of reserves, leaving the forests, once again to the tiger. It was at the time the most ambitious conservation project attempted by any country anywhere in the world. Ranthambhore was one of the initial nine reserves included in the scheme and several villages were moved out of the park in the late 1970s.

*Future generations would be truly saddened that this century had so little foresight, so little compassion, such lack of generosity of spirit for the future that it would eliminate one of the most dramatic and beautiful animals the world has ever seen.*

**George Schaller**

A decade after the project began it appeared a resounding success. Tiger numbers in India had reportedly doubled and new forests were included every few years. The 1980s were the golden years of the project and reserves like Ranthambhore became famous the world over.

## Impending Crisis

However, behind all of this good news an impending crisis was looming. The tiger's increased visibility in Ranthambhore and other high-profile reserves encouraged complacency amongst the state forest departments that administered the reserves. Less well known National Parks in India were not subject to the same level of scrutiny and tiger numbers were repeatedly doctored on the annual counts.

Counting techniques were simplistic and lacked accuracy and near impossible figures were reported in forests across India. It increasingly became clear that many reserves existed only on paper and many forests were being pilfered of their riches by organised poaching gangs, timber organisations and criminals fronting mining operations.

## Poaching

The early 1990s saw a steady increase in the number of poaching cases and even Ranthambhore, the great success story of Project Tiger, was not immune. Over 20 tigers were reportedly poached in just a couple of years, half of the reserve's cats. The same depressing statistics were reported from many National Parks around India and once again the tiger faced a struggle to survive.

## Increased Demand

One of the reasons for this increased illegal activity was a growing demand for tiger bone for use in traditional Chinese medicine. The bone is used in a variety of medicines to cure a range of illnesses. Beside bone, body parts are often eaten as delicacies and tiger penis soup is an expensive aphrodisiac favoured by rich, inadequate males across Asia. This medicine, besides causing the murder of thousands of tigers, has been scientifically proven to have absolutely no effect on people.

The Chinese had already massacred over 3000 of their own tigers. Destroyed and slaughtered as vermin, a bounty was placed on the head of every tiger in the 1960s and 1970s by the then ruler Mao Tse-Tung. It was these Chinese tigers that had supplied the trade up until the late 1980s and when stocks ran out, India's tigers were targeted.

## Constant Pressure

Beside this high incidence of poaching, habitat destruction was adding to the pressure. India, home to more than a billion people, seemed to have little room for forests and wildlife. Villagers living on the fringe of National Parks were exhausting the environment, encroaching to illegally graze their cattle, poach deer and cut wood. Cattle grazing in reserves were subsequently taken by tigers, bringing them into conflict with man. The villagers would often take revenge by poisoning the carcass, killing the tiger and, if it was a tigress, her cubs as well.

*Opposite*
Wild tiger in a wild landscape.

Illegal grazing.

## Apathy

Officials in many forests initially dismissed these fresh threats. Basking in the supposed success of Project Tiger and not wanting the bad publicity that would ruin their bloated reputations, they swept many reports under the carpet, dismissing them as rumours or lies. Backed by apathetic local governments and ineffective, poorly administrated forest departments, wild tigers seemed to have few friends and it hurts to think how badly our species has failed this beautiful creature. Entrusted with enforcing it's right to exist, our selfishness and greed has pushed it even closer to extinction.

## Ranthambhore's Change of Fortune

Ranthambhore in the early 1990s was a depressing place. What was once the most acclaimed National Park in Asia was now a shadow of its former self. Luckily its fortunes changed for the better in 1996 when a radical new forest officer named G V Reddy was entrusted with its protection.

Patrols were increased and a once demoralised forest department was rejuvenated and purposeful, repelling villagers demanding to graze their cattle inside the park.

Ranthambhore had received a welcome blessing. Offered comprehensive protection, tiger numbers increased, once again showing that left alone the tiger is capable of reproducing rapidly, possessing an astonishing ability to bounce back in the face of extreme biotic pressure.

## Space

Tigers spread throughout the forest in the following years and new litters of cubs were commonplace in many areas of the reserve. With the population rising the problem now faced by the tigers was finding a suitable, available territory. Young male tigers in particular must quickly find a new territory upon reaching maturity as resident tigers will not tolerate intruders and, on rare occasions, may even kill them.

With space at a premium, young inexperienced tigers were forced to move to the fringes of the park, once again bringing them into conflict with man, a depressing cycle that seems to have no solution. The situation had improved immeasurably but dark clouds never seem far behind every new dawn for the tiger.

## A Wild Future?

The situation varies tremendously from country to country, forest to forest. In India, Ranthambhore and other high profile reserves offer the best hope for continuation of the species, but these areas are small, with no viable migration corridors for excess tigers to disperse through. Large reserves that can contain hundreds of tigers sadly no longer exist in India. With every tree felled, every deer poached, the pressure gradually increases on the species.

Against increasingly insurmountable odds, tigers are still with us in 2003. A quite amazing statistic when you assess the magnitude of their heinous slaughter in the brutal century that has just passed. For that we should all be thankful.

Tigers have held human beings in their thrall for thousands of years, affecting cultures and races like no other creature on earth. As apex predators they are vital, essential indicators of the health of an eco-system. Tiger forests are healthy forests, supporting life on a grand scale and enhancing the quality of life of those who live in their vicinity.

Just think, right now, as you read this, a wild tiger is roaming some far-away forest in Asia, perhaps roaring resoundingly on a clear, moonlit night. Picture it for a second. Just the thought of it gives me, and I hope you, great pleasure. Knowing these magnificent animals are out there, living and breathing, existing in our world. Imagine if we didn't have the luxury of that thought. What a great tragedy it would be, if we were to lose that vision, that dream that has captured all of our imaginations.

*If you would like to know more about the battle faced by tigers and how you can help them please contact Global Tiger Patrol, a British based charity dedicated to protecting India's remaining wild tigers.*

# GLOBAL TIGER PATROL

Global Tiger Patrol, formerly known as the Ranthambhore Trust, has been working to conserve the tiger in the wild since 1989. It is believed that there may be fewer than 5,000 tigers remaining in the wild worldwide. Initially, Global Tiger Patrol's policy was people-centred conservation in and around Ranthambhore National Park in Rajasthan, India. Working with and gaining the support and cooperation of those living in and around the tiger's habitat was seen as the best way for the future. In recent years, owing to the increase in poaching and trading in the tiger and other endangered wildlife for traditional medicines and aphrodisiacs, as well as the destruction of the habitat, numbers of tigers have diminished rapidly. GTP now funds front line protection as well, often acting in a catalytic role with seed funding.

Global Tiger Patrol mainly concentrates its work in India, as the sub-continent is home to about 55% of the world's remaining wild tigers. On the whole, funds are spent on anti-poaching support to aid forest guards with their work. Many tiger reserves are short staffed and ill-equipped – GTP provides equipment such as troop carriers, jeeps, high-speed patrol boats, jungle equipment, binoculars and training for these men, who put their lives on the line daily. GTP also supports scientific research projects and continues to work with the people living in and around the tiger's habitat to help them protect their heritage.

Global Tiger Patrol is also a founding partner of 21st Century Tiger, an alliance with the Zoological Society of London, funding wild tiger protection projects and scientific research in India, Sumatra, Malaysia, Cambodia and the Russian Far East.

**87 Newland Street, Witham, Essex CM8 1AD, UK**
Telephone: +44 (0)1376 520320 Fax: +44 (0)1376 519763
Email: globaltiger@compuserve.com
www.globaltigerpatrol.co.uk

Administered by the Ranthambhore Trust ( UK charity no 328126)

# Photographer's Notes

## Approach

I have always tried to portray Ranthambhore in an original way, incorporating the habitat into my images, showing the forest, the landscape and the lakes. I like atmosphere and contrast, moody lighting that can be manipulated. In this respect the wintertime months of December to February are superb. Tigers are easier to find in summer but the light is poor.

## Natural Behaviour

When I initially arrived in Ranthambhore my first wish was to capture a tiger on film. Once I had done that I wanted to document natural behaviour. These pictures are the most pleasing to me. Firstly for the excitement of watching a stalk or a mother with cubs. Secondly, they distinguish them from images of captive animals trained to perform for photographers. A disgusting practice that proliferates in the USA and undermines the work of professionals who, spending long hours in the field, document true behaviour and add to our knowledge of the species.

## Experience

Experience is essential if you are to photograph wild tigers successfully. Once you have watched tigers for any length of time you begin to learn their habits and can attempt to interpret their behaviour. Having an idea of what, where and when they will do things is a great advantage.

One example of this is when a tiger is walking on the tracks. Having experienced this many times, I have noted that tigers will often scent mark while patrolling their territories in this way. So when I see one approaching a prominent landmark along the roadside, I immediately tell my driver to kill the engine. This reduces the vibrations and allows me to get a steady shot, an example of which can be seen on page 42.

A second example is when watching a mother with cubs. The boisterous cubs will constantly approach and nuzzle the tigress whilst being observed. If the cubs are very young the tigress will often tolerate this, however with older cubs tigress' tend to snarl, hissing at them to respect their space and keep a distance. Anticipating this can help immensely in getting the type of pictures that you see on page 102.

So by spending time watching and studying natural behaviour you begin to build up a base of knowledge that can often be crucial during the pursuit of these rare images.

## Almost Invisible

Finding wild tigers is quite a challenge. Female tigers in Ranthambhore have home ranges of over 10sq km and males 2–3 times that size. It is often said you only see a tiger when they want you to. They have the ability to melt into the forest, disappearing like ghosts. There are, however, several methods that can help you in your search.

*Pugmarks* – When patrolling their territory's tigers often walk on the 300km of roads that weave through Ranthambhore, leaving behind tracks. They do this for two reasons. Firstly they have soft padded feet and the flat, sandy roads allow them to move through the forest unhindered by thorns or rocks.

Secondly, it is a silent means of travel. They can move through the forest without fear of snapping branches or rustling long grass, which would alert any potential prey to their whereabouts. Tigers have been tracked in Ranthambhore walking 10-15km in a night along roads.

Tracks can tell you many things including whether it is a male or female and how long ago the tiger passed through. So first thing in the morning we scour the roads for fresh tracks, hoping they will lead us to a tiger.

*Alarm Calls* – Alarm calls are the best indication of a tiger's presence in an area. A variety of species will call in alarm when catching a glimpse of a cat. The sambar deer has the loudest call, and it is often a sure-fire sign that a tiger is around. Spotted deer calls are less reliable due to their skittish nature, while a langur's sharp staccato cough is also a good sign of a prowling predator. Their elevated position in the treetops allows them a marvellous vantage point, and their keen eyesight means they rarely miss a tiger if it's in the area. Interestingly, their calls differ depending on whether they have spotted a tiger or a leopard.

*Roaring* – Tigers will occasionally give themselves away by roaring. Hearing a full, resonant roar is always a magical moment for me. A tiger's roar is the deepest, densest sound I have ever heard. It is so powerful that it even bounces back off rock faces, creating an echo that can be mistaken for a rival tiger roaring back.

It is at times like these, when a tiger's roar adds to the grandeur of the wilderness, that the presence and power of these cats is simply overwhelming. We have had the good fortune of finding Machali many times after hearing her roars, the tension building as the roars get louder and she comes closer and closer.

On one memorable morning we were waiting at the entrance to a nala. It was a quiet morning and I had almost fallen asleep when Machali alerted us to her presence by roaring from about 10 metres away. Considering a tiger's roar can be heard over great distances, it was a wake-up call I shall not forget!

## Landscapes

The scenic images in this study were all shot during the winter months when the light is from a different world. The lakes at dawn on a winter's morning offer unparalleled photographic opportunities, particularly when there is a low mist. Rajbagh, with its palace and palm trees, is a favoured location of mine.

## Prey

Prey Species are encountered all year round and can be found and photographed at any time, although the sambar tend to be more visible when the lakes are receding in February and March. A favourite picture of mine is the sambar with the egret on its nose on page 52.

## Equipment

The photographs in this book were made with Canon EOS 1-N, 3, 5 and 500 bodies. Lenses included 17-35mm and 70-200mm. The majority of the tiger photographs were taken with a 300mm f4 Image Stabiliser lens. This was replaced eventually with a 300mm f2.8 Image Stabiliser, the extra stop crucial to many of my pictures of Machali's second litter of cubs.

Canon's Image Stabiliser technology remarkably allows handholding down to speeds of 1/30th of a second and even less when supported with a beanbag resting on the edge of the jeep. A great advantage, this technology gives full creative freedom to the photographer and by using these smaller, lighter lenses you can react faster when things are happening. Many photographers who visit the area with big telephotos mounted on tripods miss a lot of opportunities, particularly when a tiger is moving.

## Film

For the highest quality image I use fine grain, slow speed films such as Fuji Velvia 50 and Fuji Provia 100f, occasionally up-rating to 200-400 ASA. The forest is at times very dark, especially when the tiger is most active.

Often whilst shooting you are pushing the very boundaries of photography and only occasionally when tiger, photographer and lens are all sufficiently still will you capture your image.

*Opposite*
As she attempts to defecate on the edge of the track, Machali fixes me with an icy stare.

# Acknowledgements

I was very fortunate to meet a passionate young guide called Nafis Mohammed on one of my first days in Ranthambhore. Having a good guide is essential and can make all the difference when searching for tigers. Nafis has a remarkable knowledge of the forest, and without his assistance many of these pictures would not exist. His sixth "tiger" sense has resulted in some incredible encounters – none more so than at Lambi Nala. It is a testament to his skills that this collection of images has been compiled in a relatively short space of time.

Accompanying Nafis has been my driver, Mr Singh. He and Nafis are the perfect team and compliment each other very well. Besides driving with a deep appreciation of a photographer's needs, Papu has one of the sharpest eyes for tiger I have ever seen.

I have spent time with lots of people in the park: thanks in particular to Peter Fox, with whom I shared some remarkable days, and Bryan Angelinetta, for his good grace during an initial three weeks of abysmal tiger sighting. Ranthambhore, as I often told him, rarely disappoints.

Also in Ranthambhore: M D Parashar for his eloquent foreword, Aditya and Poonam Singh for their fine hospitality and constant e-mails, Aravind and Ravindra Jain for their kindness, Mohan Singh for his dedication and G.V Reddy for the remarkable job he did rejuvenating the reserve and for allowing me special permissions which helped enormously in obtaining the material for this book.

In New Delhi: Ananda Banerjee for his knowledge, assistance and hospitality and Vikram Singh at Wild World India for his kind help.

At home in the UK my family have offered unwavering support for what, at times, has seemed like an absurd career choice! My partner Kath has helped enormously with every aspect of this entire study, and recently found out what all the fuss was about when she experienced Ranthambhore for the first time.

I would also like to thank Amanda Bright and all at Global Tiger Patrol. I hope and expect this book will encourage others to support their crucial work. If we do nothing, it might be that pictures in books like this are all that is left of India's jungles.

My agency, Ardea, has been inundated with countless requests for slides and scans over the past few months, and has somehow managed to reunite me with most of the images in record time. In particular, I would like to thank Angela Blackwood-Murray.

Colin Woods has superbly designed and maintained my web sites, at times from the other side of the world. His patience knows no bounds.

A final thanks to Tim Scollary, whom I had the good fortune of meeting in one of those chance encounters that are often catalysts for projects such as this one. Without his enthusiasm, support and passion this celebration of Ranthambhore would not have been possible.

## Contacts

Chris Brunskill's Web-Site

www.chrisbrunskill.co.uk

Tiger Forest Web-Site

www.ranthambhore.info

Ranthambhore School of Art

http://www.artforsurvival.org/core_pages/ranathambhore.shtml

Dragonfly on cactus branch.

Bas